Be...
Se...
Battle

John Coldwell

Illustrated by Doffy Weir

OXFORD

Twins

Bertha and Fiona were twin sisters.
They looked exactly the same. There
was only one way to tell them apart.
Bertha dyed her hair red and Fiona
dyed her hair blonde. The twins lived
together in a cottage.

On Friday evenings they set off for
work at the Town Hall.

A sign outside the Town Hall said,
'Grand Wrestling Competition.'

The referee stepped under the top rope and into the ring. 'Ladies and gentlemen. Silence please for tonight's star fight.'

The doors of the dressing room swung open.

'And here she is,' cried the referee. 'The darling of the ring. Fairplay Fiona!'

A cheer went up from the crowd.
Fiona, dressed in pink, came into the
hall. Her blonde hair streamed behind
her. With one leap she jumped over
the top rope and landed in the ring.

She waved to the crowd and blew
them kisses. The crowd stood and
clapped. They wanted Fiona to win.

The referee spoke again. 'And her
opponent for tonight is...'

The dressing room doors smashed
open. One door came off its hinges.

'Her terrible twin sister. Big Bertha
the Bone Cruncher!'

Bertha, dressed in black, came into
the hall. Her red hair streamed behind
her. She took a flying leap into the
ring. She shook her fist. The crowd
booed. They wanted Bertha to lose.

The referee turned to check his watch.

Bertha grabbed Fiona and threw her against the ropes.

The crowd yelled at the referee.

Bertha raced back to her corner. The referee turned round.

'I haven't done anything wrong,' shouted Bertha.

The fight had begun.

Fiona bounced back with a flying drop kick.

The crowd stood up, cheering.

Bertha picked up Fiona and spun her above her head.

The crowd booed.

So it went for five rounds.

'And the winner is – Fairplay Fiona.'

The crowd cheered Fiona. They booed Bertha.

That night Bertha and Fiona sat at home drinking cocoa.

'I thought the fight went very well,' said Fiona.

'Hum,' said Bertha.

'You're not upset about the flying tail spin?'

'No.'

'The drop kick in round two?'

'No.'

'Then why are you in such a bad mood?'

Bertha began to cry.

'What's the matter?' asked Fiona.

'Well,' sobbed Bertha, 'people always cheer you and they always boo me.'

'That's because it's more fun for the crowd if I am Fairplay Fiona and you are Big Bertha the Bone Cruncher,' said Fiona.

'Couldn't we change?' said Bertha. 'You could be "Fearsome Fiona". I could be "Big-Hearted Bertha".'

'Don't be silly,' said Fiona. 'Besides, you are good at being bad.'

'You could teach me how to be good,' said Bertha. 'And I could teach you how to be bad.'

'No!' said Fiona. 'What would my fans think?'

Bertha fights back

Next Friday morning, after breakfast, the twins went into the front room. They put the table and chairs in a pile at one end of the room. They moved the television, the goldfish bowl and their books into the kitchen.

When the room was completely clear, Fiona said, 'Ready?'

'Ready,' said Bertha.

Then the twins began to fight. Bertha threw Fiona across the room. Fiona did a perfect cartwheel and landed lightly on her feet.

The twins always practised for the fight on Friday night. Both twins were very skilled at wrestling. They worked hard to make sure they could do their moves without hurting each other.

When they had finished practising they had to tidy the cottage and have lunch. The twins liked cooking but they hated housework. They tossed a coin to see who should tidy up.

'Heads,' said Bertha.

'Tails,' said Fiona. 'I win.'

So Bertha had to move all the things from the kitchen back into the front room. Then she had to put the table and chairs back in the middle of the room. Meanwhile, Fiona cooked lunch.

After lunch Bertha slipped quietly
into the bathroom and locked the door.
Bertha rinsed her hair with her sister's
blonde hair colour. She looked in the
mirror and smiled. Her hair was now
blonde, just like Fiona's. She poured the
rest of the blonde hair colour down the
sink. Then she filled the bottle with
some of her red hair colour.

Fiona tapped on the door. 'Hurry up in there,' she called.

'Nearly finished,' replied Bertha.

'I must colour my hair before I go jogging,' said Fiona.

Bertha came out of the bathroom. She had a towel wrapped around her head.

'I feel much better,' said Bertha. 'I've left the bathroom tidy.'

'Look at the time,' said Fiona. 'I shall be late.'

Fiona dashed into the bathroom. She splashed on her hair colour. She was in such a hurry that she did not look in the mirror.

'Have a lovely run,' said Bertha.

Fiona jogged down the road.

She ran through the park. Fiona saw a kitten sitting on a wall.

'Hello, little kitty.'

She stretched out to stroke the kitten. The kitten ran up a tree.

A policeman was passing by. 'I saw you frighten that kitten. What an unkind thing to do.'

'I only tried to stroke it,' mumbled Fiona.

'I don't believe you. I know what you're like,' the policeman replied.

Fiona jogged on towards the
playground. Some children were
playing on the swings.

'Would you like a push?' she called.

The children thought that Fiona was
Bertha. They jumped off the swings and
ran away.

The park keeper raced up. 'What do
you think you are doing? You were
chasing those children. Go and chase
someone your own size.'

Fiona ran off.

19

Fiona stopped for a rest outside
the supermarket. An old lady was
pushing her trolley towards the door.

Fiona ran over to help. She held
open the door. 'After you,' she said.

'It's a trick. I've seen you in the
wrestling ring. You are going to shut
the door in my face,' said the old lady.

The manager arrived. 'Stop
frightening my customers. Clear off
before I call the police.'

Fiona could not understand it. Why didn't people like her any more? She jogged sadly back to the cottage.

Bertha was in the garden.

'What have you done to your hair?' cried Fiona.

'Do you like it?' asked Bertha.

'It's blonde. That's my hair colour,' said Fiona.

'Is it really?' said Bertha. She took a
mirror from her pocket. She held it up
to Fiona.

'My hair!' screamed Fiona. 'It's red!
But that's your colour.'

'I know,' said Bertha.

'Everybody will think that I am you,'
said Fiona.

'That's right,' giggled Bertha.

'I will have to do my hair all over again,' said Fiona.

'You can't,' replied Bertha.

'Why not?' asked Fiona.

'Because I tipped your hair colour down the sink,' said Bertha.

'But we are due at the Town Hall in ten minutes,' moaned Fiona. 'What are we going to do?'

Heads or tails?

The Town Hall was packed with people waiting to see the big fight.

The referee stepped forward. 'Ladies and gentlemen. In the red corner: Fairplay Fiona.'

Bertha, dressed in pink with her blonde hair flying, raced forward and jumped into the ring. She waved to the crowd. Everybody cheered.

'And in the blue corner is that monster of the ring, Big Bertha the Bone Cruncher.'

Fiona, dressed in black with red hair streaming, crashed her way towards the ring. She shook her fist at Bertha.

The crowd thought that she was shaking her fist at them. They booed.

The fight began. Fiona and Bertha gripped each other by the shoulders.

'How do you like being the bad one?' hissed Bertha.

'It's horrible,' said Fiona. 'Everybody wants me to lose.'

'Now you know how I feel,' whispered Bertha. 'Right. I'm going to throw you over my shoulder.'

And that is just what she did. The crowd cheered. Bertha waved at the crowd and smiled.

'And the winner is Fairplay Fiona.'
Bertha, with blonde hair and dressed in
pink, waved. The crowd cheered.

The two sisters sat in the dressing
room as the crowd went home.

'I don't know why you're looking so
pleased with yourself,' said Fiona.

'Because I won,' said Bertha.

'But you didn't win,' said
Fiona. 'The referee said that the
winner was Fairplay Fiona.
And that's me.'

'Oh,' said Bertha.

There was a
knock on the door.

'Come in,' called Fiona.

A little man carrying an enormous
bunch of flowers slid shyly into the
dressing room.

'I've brought some flowers for Bertha,'
he said. 'You're my favourite wrestler - I
think you're wonderful. I know you're
not really a bone cruncher.'

'How kind,' smiled Bertha.

The man walked past Bertha and
handed the flowers to Fiona.

Then he went very red and ran out of
the room.

'Did you hear that?' said Bertha,
taking the flowers from Fiona. 'He thinks
I'm wonderful! He knows it's all just an
act.'

'Hey', said Fiona. 'He gave those
flowers to me!'

'Yes, because he thought you were me.
Listen,' Bertha said excitedly. 'I have an
idea that should keep everyone happy.'

'Let's hear it then,' said Fiona.

'Every Friday,' said Bertha, 'we toss a coin to see which one of us dyes their hair red and which one dyes their hair blonde.'

'No,' said Fiona. 'I can't agree to that.'

'In that case,' said Bertha, 'I shall keep my hair blonde. Then we can both be Fairplay Fiona. Nobody will come to watch two Fionas fighting. So we won't get paid. Then we will have to sell the cottage. Then…'

'All right, all right,' sighed Fiona. 'I agree.'

And so every Friday the two sisters clear the front room and practise their moves. Then they toss a coin to decide who has to do the housework. And after lunch they toss the coin again to decide their hair colour.

Sometimes it is Bertha with blonde hair and Fiona with red hair. Sometimes it is Fiona with blonde hair and Bertha with red hair. And nobody in the crowds that come to watch them fight has ever noticed.

About the author

I was born in London in 1950 and now live by the seaside, in Ramsgate. In the evening I like to write stories and poems. I do this very quietly. Then I go downstairs and play jazz records very loudly. 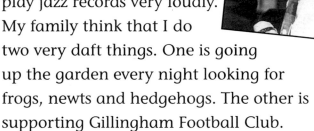 My family think that I do two very daft things. One is going up the garden every night looking for frogs, newts and hedgehogs. The other is supporting Gillingham Football Club.